AF594475

IMAGES
of America
WESTBOROUGH

This real-photo postcard shows a sign from downtown Westborough located near the train station. The Westboro Board of Trade published the postcard and described the town as "one of the most beautiful in New England. Westboro is rated as being one of the most healthy towns in the State. It is now and always been a no license town, and is orderly and progressive." (Author's collection.)

On the Cover: The Wednesday Club is shown on a picnic in this 1880s image. On the left, a banjo player is strumming his tunes; Mrs. Charles Fay is behind the spinning wheel, while her husband lies on the grass. Villagers met in many different social clubs and groups to pass away the time. (Author's collection.)

Philip M. Kittredge

ISBN 978-1-4671-0532-3

Published by Arcadia Publishing
Charleston, South Carolina

Printed in the United States of America

Library of Congress Control Number: 2020932418

For all general information, please contact Arcadia Publishing:
Telephone 843-853-2070
Fax 843-853-0044
E-mail sales@arcadiapublishing.com
For customer service and orders:
Toll-Free 1-888-313-2665

Visit us on the Internet at www.arcadiapublishing.com

This book is dedicated to my wife, Donna, who is the love of my life, and my two beautiful daughters, Kagan and Shannon.

Contents

Acknowledgments

My collection of images started more than 50 years ago because of Donald Lowe of the Lowe's Variety Store family. He wrote a local history column for the newspaper, and I began reading it every week. I became obsessed and soon started collecting anything I could find about Westborough. My collection now contains many original images, postcards, stereoviews, and glass negatives. My intent is for the entire collection to be donated to the Westborough Library and be available for residents to view or copy. Many of the images have been used in various books over the years. The most notable was *On the Beaten Path* by Kristina Allen. Published in 1984, this long out-of-print book remains the definitive writing about Westborough history and is available at the Westborough Public Library. I owe a great debt of gratitude to Mrs. Allen for reviewing the text and images in this book for historical accuracy. Author Katherine Anderson was another important factor in the production of this book. We spent much time reviewing images for her book on Westborough State Hospital that was published in 2019. Her enthusiasm for that subject was contagious and helped convince me that the time was right for this book on Westborough.

Caroline Anderson, my title manager at Arcadia Publishing, has been a constant source of encouragement. She reviewed all the digital images submitted each week and determined if they met the quality standards required for publication. Her feedback and encouragement were especially helpful in the beginning, when this seemed like such an enormous task.

The most important person in the production of this book is my wife, Donna. She was invaluable in her editing of the finished manuscript and has spent countless hours retyping my text and correcting grammar and spelling. I could not have done it without her.

All images in this book appear courtesy of my personal collection.

Introduction

Westborough celebrated its 300th anniversary in 2017, but Westborough's roots began in 1659 at Chauncy Pond. It was originally part of Marlborough and known as the Village of Chauncy. By 1668, the strong-willed people of Chauncy had a major influence on the town of Marlborough, and the town was not responsive to the needs or wishes of the new village. The village petitioned the General Court in 1702 to be separated from Marlborough, but it was denied. In 1717, another petition was filed successfully, and the village was incorporated as the Town of Westborough. Westborough was the 100th town to be incorporated in Massachusetts. According to published records, the earliest residents were farmers who, in order to survive, had to battle Native Americans, wolves, wildcats, and rattlesnakes.

Today, Westborough has different neighbors than when it was originally incorporated. In 1717, Lancaster was the town's neighbor to the north, Marlborough to the east, Mendon and Sutton to the south, and Worcester and Brookfield to the west.

According to the diary of Rev. Ebenezer Parkman, the first minister of Westborough, there were 25 heads of families and 6 young men in 1724. The arrival of the Boston & Worcester Railroad in 1834 forever changed the character of the town. The Boston-Worcester Turnpike was only 25 years old, and the railroad ultimately forced the relocation of commerce to the center of town. By 1839, there were 50 houses in the village and a population of 1,612 people. In 1875, a total of 451,591 gallons of milk were produced and shipped to Boston via the railroad. By 1879, about 800,000 gallons of milk were shipped from Westborough and from neighboring towns each year. Agriculture remained important, with 4,500 acres under active cultivation, but times were changing. The United States was entering the Gilded Age, and Westborough went along for the ride. As the 20th century drew closer, industry developed in unprecedented numbers. Factories arose and produced various items ranging from sleighs to straw hats. The Locomobile, pianos, bicycles, boots, and shoes were all produced and shipped out from the large Westborough rail yard. Small dry goods shops and hardware stores started to occupy the newly constructed buildings in the downtown area. Barbers, druggists, butchers, and bakers found a ready clientele among the thousands of local workers.

In 1889, the Westborough Board of Trade published a broadside with village information. The following was printed under the heading of population: "The population is about 6000 [In reality, it would take 30 more years to reach that number.] The industries employ an excellent class of help. The standard of intelligence and prosperity is very high. Palaces and hovels are both lacking. The dwellings betoken general thrift and comfortable homes."

It was around this time, in 1894, that the town's name was officially changed to Westboro. In 1717, the incorporated name of Westborough was derived from the area being the west "borough," or section, of Marlborough. Local businesses shortened the official name to Westboro, with an apostrophe at the end, and Westborough soon became Westboro'. It was only natural that the shortened name became preferred. This all changed in 1971, when Westborough returned as the official spelling as approved by the US Department of the Interior. Both spellings remain popular and are still in use today by local merchants.

After the end of World War I and the start of the Roaring Twenties, women helped drive the economy of the town. They were liberated, gained the right to vote, and became employed in the factories and stores. Many of them settled in Westborough, but the population still remained under 6,000.

During World War II, the town did its share for the war effort through manufacturing. All of the US military paratroopers had mukluks produced by the Rasmussen Shoe Company. Most of the male workers who were employed at the Westborough Tannery on Beach Street were called up to join the war effort. Due to the loss of men working in the factories, women had to step up and perform the men's jobs until they returned from the war. The tannery's owner, James Cooper, produced a monthly newsletter that he mailed to employees fighting the war. "Tannery Trimmings" gave updates on the employees' fellow workers; in addition to war news, local events, births, and deaths were included in every issue. Sometimes the news was discouraging, but it provided a sense of family for the soldiers. The newsletter was produced every month until the war ended. With the war over and soldiers coming home, all were welcomed back with parades and celebrations. An upsurge of homes being built brought many new families to town following the postwar residential boom. Industry continued to grow and provided plenty of jobs for locals. The population increased by almost 50 percent—to just under 10,000—by 1960.

The town changed dramatically from the 1960s through 1980. Many of the small farms started to vanish, and large housing tracts, as well as imposing apartment buildings, started to appear on the landscape. In 20 years, approximately 2,000 apartments were built. Shopping centers were constructed on Route 9, causing great concern about the future of downtown businesses. Residences were needed for the aging population, so private and public housing was built. The Evergreen Rest Home on East Main Street closed, and large multifloor nursing homes arrived.

The Westborough School District also responded to the change in population with the construction of three new schools. Annie E. Fales Elementary School was built in 1963 for $900,000. Westborough High School was constructed at the site of the former Aronson Property on West Main Street in 1968. The $4 million school was built to house 1,000 students. The 30-acre property had been damaged, and the home had been destroyed in the 1953 tornado. Elsie A. Hastings Elementary School opened in 1970, and cost in excess of $2 million. Westborough became part of the Assabet Vocational Region, a new vocational school constructed in 1970. In 2001, Mill Pond School was constructed, and a large addition—plus renovations to the high school—were completed that same year. A replacement to the Annie E. Fales School is scheduled to be completed in 2021.

In the 2010s, the town renovated the town hall, Forbes Municipal Building, and police department and constructed a new fire station to keep up with increased demands.

This book focuses on Westborough in the Gilded Age. Most of these images are from original glass negatives from between 1870 and 1920 that have been restored and then digitized. Their condition appears as impressive today as it did when the images were captured more than 100 years ago. The glass negatives can be as large as 11 by 14 inches or as small as 4 by 6 inches. Westborough was well represented in this collection, as there were at least fifteen professional photographers operating in town. Most people have seen representations of the old-time photographer with a camera resting on a large tripod and a hood he used to cover his head and shoulders in order to block out the light; this is how these photographs were taken.

All of the images in this book come from the author's collection, which includes several thousand images of Westborough, including lantern slides, stereoscopic views, real-photo postcards, and lithographs.

One

A Village Worships

After the incorporation of Westborough in 1717, local government and religion were closely associated. The year 1825 was the beginning of separate structures for worship and town government. At that time, the First Congregational Society was organized. In the following years, additional churches were constructed, and by 2019, Westborough had 13 diverse houses of worship.

In 1748, voters approved the construction of the Second Meeting House on the corner of West Main and Milk Street. Town meetings and church services were conducted there until 1837, when the building was sold. The new owner quickly removed the steeple, and the structure was renamed the Arcade Building. The building was then raised, and a new first floor was constructed. Meeting rooms were located upstairs, with several small shops on the first floor and basement levels.

In 1890, the Arcade Building was demolished, as it was found to be in poor condition. A new brick building was then constructed on the same site and remained known as the Arcade. In 2018, the building underwent a complete restoration to the storefronts and is now the central point of downtown Westborough.

The Evangelical Congregational Church was constructed in 1834 at the corner of West Main and Church Streets. In a move similar to what happened with the Second Meeting House, the entire church was raised up by hand, and additional rooms and a basement were added in 1869.

In 1869, the Evangelical Congregational Church interior was entirely remodeled. This real-photo postcard from around 1910 shows the front of the church prior to another change. The organ was moved from the back section of the church to the front.

The entire front of the Evangelical Congregational Church was redesigned. The altar was remodeled and pushed forward, closer to the pews. A new platform was constructed to make room for a new organ and choir loft.

The new pipe organ was installed at the front of the Evangelical Congregational Church, and a wall was erected to form the new choir loft. The view of the altar was made more appealing by the removal of the large recessed opening, and the doors were hidden from sight.

The First Baptist Society formed a few years prior to the organization of the First Baptist Church in 1814. The original church was raised and moved to the corner of Milk and Phillips Streets after being sold to the Westborough Catholic Parish; it was destroyed by fire in 1886. The pictured church replaced the original church on this site at 36 West Main Street in 1869. The two organizations merged in 1890, around the time this photograph was taken. Due to declining membership, the Westborough Baptist Church closed its doors in 2007, and the building was sold in 2012.

The First United Methodist Church built its first church at 30 Milk Street in 1864. The congregation had been worshipping at the High School House next to Memorial Cemetery on West Main Street. Due to multiple complaints from members about the noise from the trains running past the front door of the church, the building was sold to the Westborough Grange in 1897. The building is now home to the New Hope Chapel.

The Second Advent congregation sold its church at 12 Church Street to the Methodist Society. After extensive renovations, the new Methodist church was opened in 1900. The building was sold to Siloam Masonic Lodge in 1966. The new Methodist church was built in 1968 at 129 West Main Street.

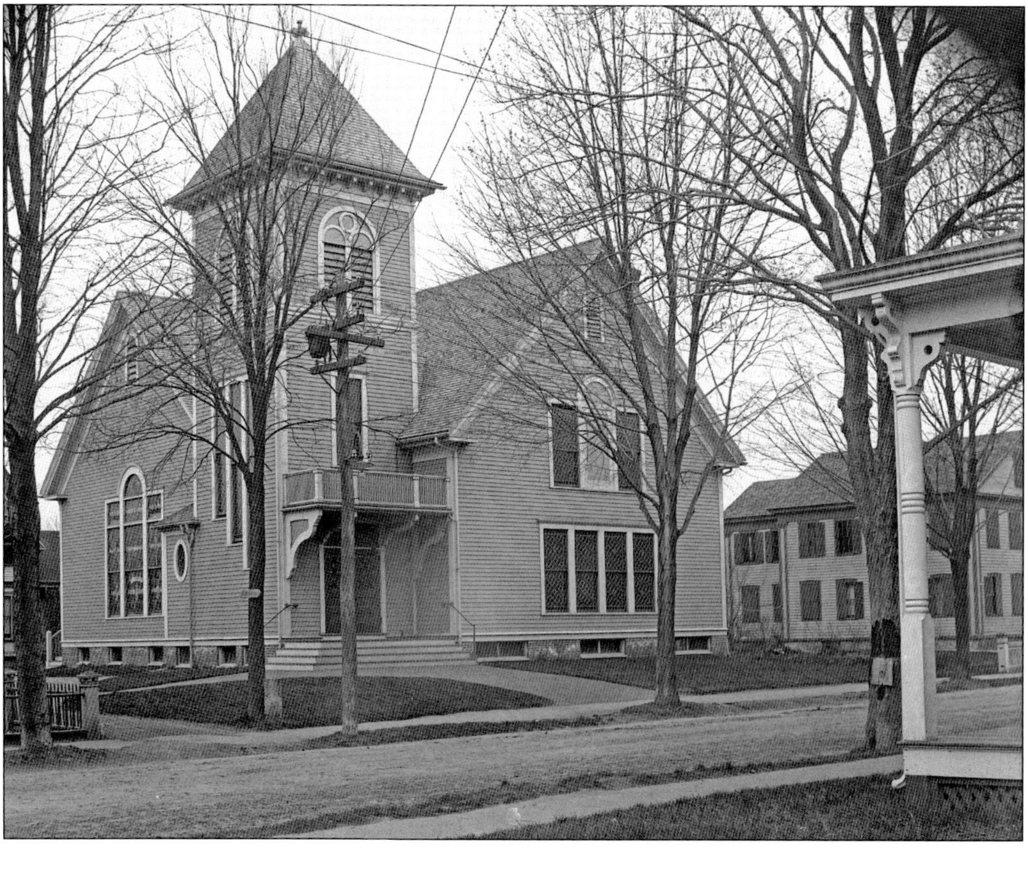

The St. Luke the Evangelist Church was initially located on Milk Street near Phillips Street; unfortunately, the wooden structure was destroyed by fire in 1886. In 1888, the new St. Luke the Evangelist Church was built at 70 West Main Street, and a rectory next door soon followed. Unfortunately, this church was also destroyed by fire in 1920. In 1921, the current church was constructed on the same site; this time, it was made of brick.

St. Luke the Evangelist Church was large and looked impressive from the outside. The First Congregational Unitarian Universalist Society next door was half the size. The large influx of factory workers from Ireland and Italy were mostly Catholic, and this is where they worshipped. By the mid-1850s, there were almost 500 Catholics living in Westborough.

The interior of St. Luke the Evangelist was even more impressive than the outside. Spectacular cathedral-style plaster columns rose 30 feet to arched ceilings. The ornate altar was framed by three large stained-glass windows. Numerous large stained-glass windows that flanked the walls leading to each side of the altar let in a lot of light.

The First Congregational Unitarian/Universalist Society built its church at 64 West Main Street. Construction was completed in 1849, and the church was dedicated in 1850. Thirty years later, the chapel was constructed. As in other town buildings, dangerous gas lamps were removed and replaced with electric lights in 1895.

Two

LAUGHTER AT THE LAKE

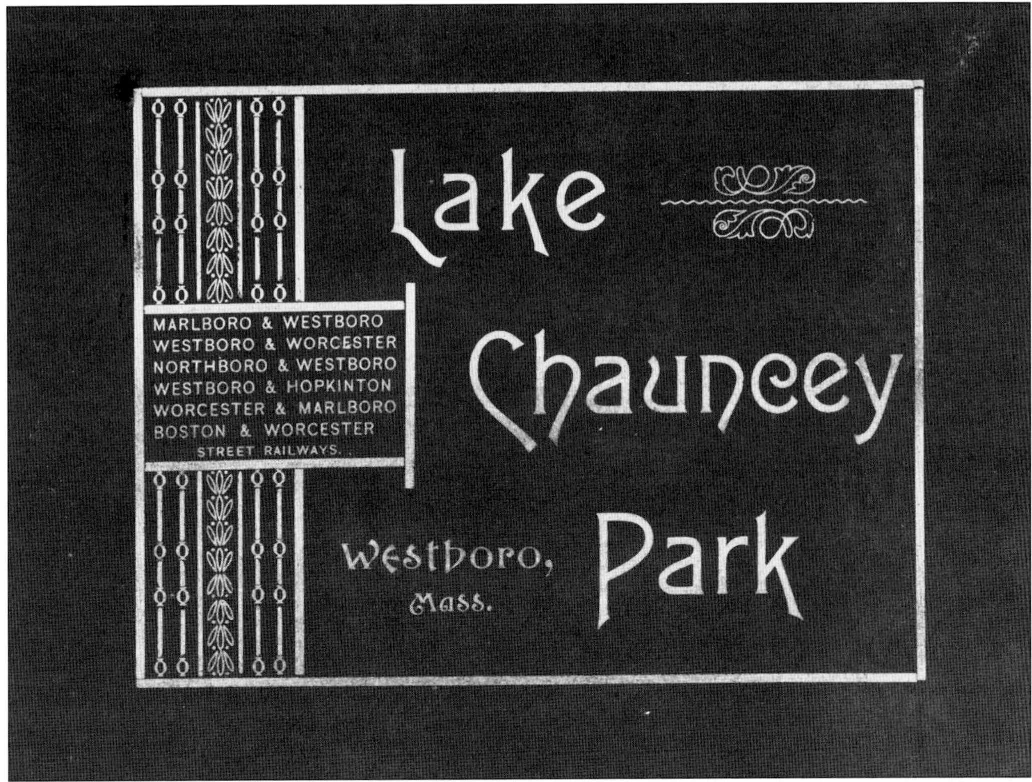

Lake Chauncy, located near the town's northern boundary, is Westborough's largest body of water. It encompasses 178 acres of pine groves and sparkling water. Lake Chauncy Park opened in 1876, and in 1901, it was purchased by the Worcester Consolidated Street Railway Company. Streetcars brought visitors from surrounding towns to relax and enjoy the many attractions. Along with boat and canoe rentals, the lake offered many other attractions that kept visitors entertained.

The trolley companies ran special streetcars just for Chauncy Park. It cost a nickel to ride from the center of town to the park. After guests arrived, they could partake in various activities, such as enjoying a play at the outdoor theater, watching moving-picture shows that were conducted every evening, or renting various sizes of boats for a scenic paddle around the lake. Three nights per week, gentlemen could take their ladies to the dance hall for a spin around the floor.

Chauncy Park was well-known for having a wonderful picnic area. Guests arrived early in the morning and did not leave until late in the evening. They found the cool breeze off the lake in the summer very refreshing and could quench their thirst at the beer garden. Many churches hosted lunches for their parishioners at the lake. Near the bowling alleys, there was a refreshment stand where New England's favorite soft drink, Moxie, could be purchased along with other snacks.

Numerous factories conducted outings at the park for their valued employees. In addition to the picnic area, guests could enjoy a game of baseball, engage in a lively game of horseshoes, go bowling, or just enjoy the playground area with the swings. It was an ideal way to relax after a hard week of work.

The park had a wonderful outdoor theater. A piano player provided musical accompaniment for the actors who came from as far away as Boston to perform here. With the arrival of moving pictures, a new permanent building was erected in which guests could watch movies for 10¢. Even vaudeville shows were performed here.

A wooden sign leaning on the telephone pole outside of Woodman's Store on West Main Street announced important information about the latest play at the Chauncy Theater. In this photograph, it reads: "Lake Chauncy Theater, last day today of *The Midnight Express*—Monday Night." The only mention of this play is in a trade magazine from 1904; no local media contained word of it.

The dance pavilion (to the right in this photograph) could hold up to 2,000 happy dancers. The Street Railway Company advertised the pavilion as follows: "A spacious hall surrounded by a broad covered veranda bountifully supplied with seats and brilliantly illuminated with myriads of incandescent electric lights, where the non-dancer can sit and listen to the dreamy sounds of a six-piece orchestra."

In later years, the dance pavilion was transformed into a large roller-skating rink during the day, but at night, it once again became the dance hall. Visitors arrived by trolley—and later, by bus—to dance the night away. Unfortunately, a devastating fire in 1949 destroyed most of the park's buildings, including the pavilion.

Of course, the water was one of the other main attractions at the park. Canoes and rowboats could be rented by the hour from several boathouses. For a small fee, passengers could even explore the lake on a steam-powered tour boat that had a colorful canopy to protect them from the sun. "No Loafing," said the signs on the building next to this boathouse.

Starting in 1714, the Forbes family had multiple homes in Westborough. The family owned the only large summerhouse on the lake, located at 15 Chauncy Street, which was constructed around 1905. The family's descendants were all successful and highly philanthropic. The family built or financially assisted in the construction of many town buildings that bear their name. The Forbes Municipal Building (formerly Westborough High School), Forbes Community House, and the current town hall were all constructed with assistance from the Forbes family.

The Forbes summerhouse provided the best views of the lake. Sunsets could be observed from the small stone pavilion at the water's edge. Directly across the lake was the Westborough Insane Asylum, which was brightly illuminated by electric lights powered by the asylum's own coal-fired generating station. The generating station is one of the last remaining asylum buildings.

The Westborough Insane Asylum took over the buildings and grounds of the former state reform school in 1884. After two years of construction and renovations, the facility opened in 1886 with 200 patients. The hospital had its own beach and bathhouse on the north side of the lake for patient and staff use. The hospital also obtained its drinking water from the lake until 1909.

The Westborough Board of Trade formed in 1890. The main object of the association was "to encourage and promote the growth of manufacturers and other industries within the town of Westborough." They held annual road races that ended at Lake Chauncy with a community field day and celebration.

Mason Taft had the only icehouse at the lake; it was located on Lyman Street near Chauncy Street. A segment of the original building is visible in this c. 1895 image. A much larger building was constructed about 10 years later. Ice harvested from the lake was packed away in the building and insulated by straw and sawdust. Ice could last for up to a year in these types of icehouses.

This c. 1905 view shows the much larger icehouse in operation. Once the ice was approximately one foot thick, icemen would cut it into blocks. A team of horses would drag the ice blocks to the base of the icehouse, where additional horses would haul the ice up the ramps and into the building. In 1913, refrigerators were invented for home use, and shortly after that, the icehouse became obsolete.

Three

STATE REFORM SCHOOL

In 1846, citizens and magistrates brought forth a petition asking for a state institution for juvenile offenders. Several months later, Gov. George Nixon Briggs appointed commissioners to purchase land, erect a building, and establish a system for the reformation of child criminals. One year later, the state purchased the 180-acre Lovett Peters farm on the northern shores of Chauncy Pond. The initial building, pictured here, was finished in 1848 and housed 310 boys. Former governor Theodore Lyman donated $30,000 toward the original purchase and construction of the facility.

Shortly after the reform school opened, a second farm and more land were purchased, bringing the site to just over 280 acres. In 1853, several large buildings were constructed to house an additional 250 boys. The new buildings contained a chapel, classrooms, a hospital, and accommodations for the staff. In addition, a workshop was constructed in a separate area, as well as 20 cells for the more difficult boys.

The new buildings were impressive and functional, constructed with large windows to let in sunlight and fresh air; they were heated by a furnace instead of coal stoves. In 1859, most of the buildings and the chapel were nearly destroyed in a fire set by an inmate. The structures were rebuilt, and three houses—where the most trustworthy boys were allowed to reside—were constructed.

The 1859 fire started in a ventilation shaft and spread to the attic. Fire departments from surrounding towns worked for almost two days to fully extinguish the fire. The reform school had its own fire equipment, which allowed the boys to provide assistance at the fire. The Lyman Fire Engine Company was equipped with a small hose cart and a New York–style hand tub, which was pulled to the fire and operated by 16 inmates.

A new building addition held the reform school's chapel and was located east of the original building. Services were held every morning and evening, and Sunday school was taught by ministers from the local churches. The chapel, with its balcony, was large enough to seat all 600 boys. The chapel was unique among other areas of the school, as it was heated by a furnace.

The kitchen was large and efficient, with multiple wall ovens. The ovens were fueled by a single source that provided heat for baking, cooking, and heating water. The staff had to prepare approximately 2,000 meals per day. In 1854, all of the operations of the farm were transferred to the Department of Agriculture, which would pay the school 10¢ per day for each boy who worked. By 1857, more than 200 boys were working on the farm and raising most of the fruits and vegetables used in the school's meals as well as tending to the livestock.

In the first few years of the farm, daily work for the boys included preparing the fields for crops, building stone walls, and trenching the gardens. Fruits, vegetables, milk, pork, and beef were all produced on the farm. A piggery, slaughterhouse, and multiple barns were constructed. Fertilizer came from the solid waste from the school that was then dried and made into a liquid to be spread on the hay fields. This picture shows the boys working in the potato field in 1875.

The boys ate on pewter plates and drank from pewter cups in the large, airy dining room. They ate in shifts, with the younger children eating first. The daily schedule was strict and started at 5:00 a.m. Breakfast was served from 6:00 to 7:00 a.m., lunch from 12:00 to 1:00 p.m., and dinner from 4:00 to 5:00 p.m. During the day, the boys were expected to attend religious exercise in the morning. Education classes were held from 10:00 a.m. to noon and 5:00 to 7:00 p.m.; work took up the rest of the day.

There were four grades at the school. The first grade was for beginners in reading. Second grade was for students who could read simple words and were taught spelling. In the third grade, students were taught reading, spelling, arithmetic, and geography. Students who were proficient in reading and spelling were placed in the fourth grade, where they also studied arithmetic, geography, and grammar. These grading systems changed and evolved over time.

The reform school had its own hospital and staff. A local doctor would visit once per week to check on any problems and would instruct the nurse and staff about required treatments. In the 36 years the school was in operation, there were approximately 75 boys who died from illness or disease. In 1858, a cemetery was built, along with a receiving tomb. Prior to an inmate being buried, a service was held in the chapel before the coffin was placed on a wagon and transported the quarter mile to the cemetery. The exact location of the cemetery is unknown.

Most of the boys' days consisted of manual labor. The younger boys worked in the sewing shop learning how to sew and make all the clothing for the inmates. As at the state hospital, the boys made all the washcloths, towels, blankets, and bed linens. The older boys worked in the fields, the shoe shop, or the chair shop to learn a trade. The goal was to provide the boys with the means to acquire personal independence. Many of the boys continued in the trades they learned after they left school.

The new addition to the building had an area called "the Lodge," which had individual cells to house the tougher, more difficult boys. After working eight hours in the workshop, the boys would return to their cells to eat meals, read, and sleep. For the safety of the younger or less problematic inmates, these boys were segregated from the rest of the population. Twice a day, they would be escorted to the yard for fresh air and relaxation.

Most of the boys spent time outside, as fresh air was thought to help cleanse the mind and build character. There were many different activities to help them pass the time, including football, horseshoes, and other outside sports. There were special groups available for the boys to join depending on their behavior.

The school had a marching band; one of the marching band units was called the Lyman Cadet Corps. Usually, cadet corps were found in military schools, so it was unique to find a unit in a reform school. The Lyman Cadet Corps participated in local parades and performed for the residents of Westborough.

Not every boy found his way into one of the elite groups like the marching band, which was usually reserved for older boys who had earned the privilege. As the older boys aged out of the system and were released, younger boys were able to apply for the coveted positions.

Of course, there was always time for America's relatively new pastime, baseball, which the older boys were allowed to play in the courtyard. According to historians, baseball was developed by the New York Knickerbocker Baseball Club in 1846. The Lovett Peters farmhouse is shown in the background in this c. 1875 view.

This picture of the original Lovett Peters farmhouse is from about 1875. This farmhouse and barns were part of the original purchase of land and property for the school. The house and barns were in such good, habitable condition that they were used by staff for housing and meals. Eventually, dinners were served in the house for boys who earned that privilege.

Allen G. Shepard was superintendent of the school from 1874 through 1879. He and his wife are shown relaxing in the parlor of the Peters farm building. Luxurious furnishings and fine art were typical for a person with his responsibilities.

The offices in the new addition that was built after the fire in 1859 were bright and airy because of large windows. The abundant, bright sunlight and fresh air were especially appreciated in the summer. During the winter months, steam heat kept the office temperature comfortable. The cat (at right) appears to be enjoying the steam radiators shown in this image. Gas being produced on the property by a generator enabled gas fixtures to illuminate the entire building. All of these new buildings and features were short-lived, however, as the school was deemed a failure and moved to the Powder Hill and Wessonville part of Westborough in 1884; it was then renamed the Lyman School for Boys.

Four

Lyman School for Boys

The Lyman School for Boys was established in 1885 after the state reform school was relocated. A new facility was required to house the state's children convicted of crimes. Some of the children were sent to this reform school for minor "crimes" such as truancy or being a stubborn child, while some of children were violent felons. Because all the children were incarcerated in one general population, an attempt was made to separate the youngest boys from the older ones. The new facility grew to approximately 700 acres, which allowed for large dormitories, a hospital, woodworking shops, a large printing shop, and almost 500 acres of land dedicated to farming.

The Lyman School for Boys was much different from the previous state reform school. Multiple large brick buildings, such as the Hillside Cottage (pictured), were constructed to house boys from ages 10 to 15. It was thought that living in a familial setting in buildings called cottages would encourage the boys to behave. The boys were expected to attend school and learn a trade in either the school's print shop or carpentry shop. Many excellent sleighs were manufactured at the school, and this angered local sleigh manufacturers.

All the new buildings, or cottages, were named for places of geographical importance; the names included Wayside, the Elms, Bowlder, Lyman Hall, Chauncy Hall, the Gables, Oak Cottage (pictured), and several more. The original plan was for each cottage to house a married couple supervising 25 to 30 boys.

The Gables Cottage was typical at the school. A master and matron, usually a married couple, lived in the cottage with the boys, who had sleeping areas in separate rooms away from the couple. The boys would be up by 5:00 a.m. to attend school for one hour in the morning, then they would attend for three hours in the afternoon. The boys were responsible for all the housekeeping chores in the cottage. The teacher and a laundress also lived in cottages on the property.

The school was constructed about one mile from the former reform school in an area of town referred to as Wessonville. Most of the buildings were located off Oak Street or Turnpike Road. The old Wesson Tavern was purchased and used as a cottage for the Lyman School in later years. The Wayside Cottage is pictured here sometime in the 1890s. As with most of the images for this book, this picture is taken from a glass negative.

Behind the Wayside Cottage were some of the barns for the school. One of the wagons the boys used to transport 300 tons of coal each year to provide heat and electricity for the school is visible inside the barn at right. The coal was loaded onto wagons from the railroad on Milk Street near Maynard Street. Like at the state hospital, a separate power plant provided utilities to most of the buildings through underground tunnels. The abandoned power plant still remains today.

The grounds of the Lyman School rivaled those of any private school in the commonwealth. Large tree-lined streets provided easy access to the property, as shown in this view looking from Turnpike Road up Park Street with the school in the distance. All of the buildings were connected by wide cement walkways that the boys were expected to keep clear in winter. The boys were also responsible for keeping the grass and bushes trimmed in the summer.

On the back of this postcard, which was mailed in 1915, Alice tells her mother that she tires very easily, but she is glad to be back teaching, except for the cold weather. The three windows circled (and with an arrow pointing to them) in this view of Lyman Hall–Chancy Hall indicate the room that Alice was residing while she worked at the school. There were many stories of abuse and tales of missing runaways being murdered, with their bodies buried in the swamps behind the hill. No evidence was ever found to support such wild allegations.

Irene sent this postcard view of the school building in June 1914. She writes, "I am spending five days here in Westboro. Saturday, I visited this Lyman School. It is a state school for bad boys. 400 boys are enrolled. It is most beautiful. About 8 buildings and acres of land. It is beautiful and their exhibition of work was great."

Boys at the school were expected to learn a trade whether they wanted to or not. The trades taught were grounds-keeping, laundry, cooking, carpentry, painting, masonry, janitorial work, electrical work, plumbing, boiler maintenance, and printing. Many boys received training in the basement of the cottages where they resided; this was meant to turn them into productive members of society.

The large farm allowed the boys to raise crops to help feed others at the school. The school won many awards at annual agriculture fairs sponsored by the Westborough Agricultural Society, which was among the most social of the numerous organizations in town. Each year, residents were excited about the parade and cattle exhibitions. As always, bragging rights were awarded to the farmer with the largest and most productive dairy cow.

Not all of the buildings were new; this image is the former Wesson Tavern used by the Lyman School. The commonwealth purchased additional buildings along Turnpike Road. As the school's population increased, new housing was required, and existing buildings were converted to be used as cottages. The overcrowding became worse each year, and soon, the school was over capacity. By the 1960s, the school had almost 600 students in facilities that were designed for half that number.

The school was finally closed in 1971. Unlike at the former site of the state hospital, many of the original buildings are still standing at the former school location. The administration building, shown here, is still in use by Spectrum Health Systems. The auditorium, laundry, powerhouse, and several of the cottages are still standing but are abandoned. The classroom building and cafeteria are still being used by private entities.

This picture of the Lyman School Boys' Band was taken on the steps of the Gables Cottage. The band not only marched for every parade, they also performed for the residents at Lake Chauncy on special occasions. The residents commented about how much they enjoyed the performances.

Harry Wilcox was the director of the Lyman School Boys' Band when this photograph was taken in 1913. Being selected for the band was a privilege, and the boys studied and practiced every day. In addition, the boys had to learn how to march; they practiced three times a week until Wilcox thought they were ready to perform. Being in the band was a status symbol at the school.

Five

Westborough Insane Asylum

The Westboro Insane Asylum opened its doors for patients in December 1886. Approximately 200 patients arrived here from other state facilities that were overcrowded. The location chosen for the asylum was ideal. The buildings were situated on the shores of Lake Chauncy and surrounded by meadows and fields. The facility finally closed in 2010, and the 12 remaining patients from the hearing-impaired unit were transferred to other facilities that could address their needs. All of the original buildings have been demolished in anticipation of a new active adult community housing project. The planned project will consist of 14 buildings containing over 700 units.

The main entrance to the asylum was located off Lyman Street, where a small, unassuming stone entrance led to the administration building. Situated near the entrance was one of the large barns that housed some of the dairy cows. The staff and patients cared for the pigs that were raised on the property prior to being slaughtered. The milk, pork, and vegetables produced there were distributed to other state hospitals.

Most of the barns were built around 1848, when the property was owned by the state reform school. In later years, a few new barns were built at the piggery site that housed more than 5,000 pigs. One of the common problems at the asylum was fire. The town fire station was located more than two miles from the facility, which led to a prolonged response time when fires occurred. Unfortunately, this delayed response time left quite a few buildings damaged or destroyed by flames. The barn at right in the photograph was destroyed by fire on August 17, 1906, causing the loss of 13 prized dairy cows and 4 calves.

Renovations were required when the existing buildings of the former state reform school were transferred to the Massachusetts State Board of Health, Lunacy and Charity in 1884. The prison cells had been removed, a large center section was rebuilt for the needs of patients, and additional recreation space was constructed. The original hospital was designed to house approximately 500 patients, but by 1910, there were over 1,000 patients on the grounds. The adjacent property was purchased so that a number of other buildings could be quickly constructed.

NURSES HOMES AND STANLEY HOUSE - WESTBORO HOSPITAL.

Between 1907 and 1915, the Westboro Insane Asylum was officially renamed the Westborough State Hospital. Different accounts give conflicting dates. Other changes were occurring due to the large influx of patients. Staff members at the hospital who were working 10 hours a day, 6 days a week, were provided with living quarters. Doctors had their own brick building, nurses resided in three new homes, and the maintenance staff and supervisor lived in the Stanley House.

The hospital superintendent was provided with a private residence around 1905. Previously, all superintendents and their families lived in the main hospital building along with the patients. This luxurious home with covered porches and balconies was built overlooking the lake. There were a sufficient number of bedrooms and living areas for the family and staff members.

The hospital was completely independent from the town. People on the grounds raised their own livestock, with the animals supplying all the milk and eggs they could use, and they grew all their own vegetables and fruit. They had their own water system with wells and sewer beds. The poor quality of water drawn from wells and the lake required a change to the municipal water supply. The large metal water tank visible here was replaced with a new granite water tower after it was connected to the Metropolitan Water System in 1909.

Dwarfing the administration building, a new water tower constructed from pink granite quarried in Milford, Massachusetts, replaced the rusty metal tower. With its ability to store uncontaminated freshwater, the new tower could supply the hospital's growing needs.

Ethel sent this postcard of the Talbot Building on March 22, 1909. She wrote, "I am painting here almost every day. I shall never forget those lovely pansy's you painted. Will see you at the club soon. With love to all. Ethel." The Talbot Building was constructed in 1898. It offered a refreshing change with its large windows and rooms constructed to provide a maximum amount of sunlight and fresh air.

Codman Hall was constructed a few years after the Talbot Building. Located on the east side of the campus, Codman Hall was a large, imposing structure that also had big windows. This building housed the acute patients who arrived at the hospital, while chronic patients remained in the original main building.

On the southern side of Lake Chauncy sat the Warren Farm. This area was renamed the Warren Colony after the hospital purchased the property around 1900. The farmhouse was remodeled for patients, and soon, two brick structures were built that were connected by underground tunnels. A small powerhouse was constructed on the shores of Lake Chauncy to supply electricity and steam heat for the buildings. Some of the buildings housed the "insane," while others housed patients suffering from tuberculosis. The buildings had solariums facing the water, which permitted bright sunlight and fresh air to enter the buildings. This treatment—fresh air and sunlight—was thought to be beneficial to those suffering from tuberculosis. The farmhouse was destroyed by arson in the late 1960s, and the brick buildings were demolished shortly afterward.

Multiple buildings made of wood and brick were constructed on the campus to meet the needs of a growing institution. As time passed, the older buildings were renovated and repurposed. The farm office and other buildings are visible along the east side of the main entrance to the hospital.

In the early 1900s, the Stanley House was renovated so patients could have access to a wonderful recreational facility where they could enjoy reading areas, billiard tables, and tennis courts. In the 1950s, it was converted for recreational purposes for the employees. A lounge and quiet area were constructed with outside seating for their comfort and enjoyment.

By 1950, there were more than 2,000 patients and 800 staff members. Additional buildings were constructed at that time and are the only buildings from the hospital campus that are still standing today. The Daniels Building and Hennessy Building have been demolished, while Paine Hall, Sharp Building, and Hadley Building are all that remain. The Department of Youth Services has several programs on the former hospital site.

The hospital always had close ties to the town. This photograph from 1912 shows the hospital float—a representative of the hospital's community involvement. Excess produce and flowers fresh from the greenhouse were available for townspeople to purchase. A nursing program was also established, and many of the graduates later became employed at the hospital.

Six

The Railroad Roars into Town

On November 15, 1834, Westborough was changed forever. The arrival of the Boston & Worcester Railroad brought industry and jobs to this quiet town. Twelve English-style coaches were filled with dignitaries on the initial three-hour trip from Boston to Westborough. This commemorative sheet music indicates the importance of this event.

The arrival of the Boston & Worcester Railroad in the downtown Westborough area created a dramatic change in the community. The Worcester Turnpike had been the primary route used to deliver passengers and freight to the town. Unfortunately, within 10 years of the arrival of the railroad, stores and taverns along the turnpike had closed. A new center of commerce had emerged, as hotels were built and numerous manufacturing and retail facilities opened near the railroad.

Westborough had a unique advantage over nearby towns regarding the railroad. Salesmen from Boston would arrive by train, find a room in one of Westborough's plentiful hotels or rooming houses, then travel to surrounding communities to conduct their business. Large buildings erected near the train station were filled with stores. Any passenger who stepped off the train would see local merchants who could fulfill their every need.

By 1870, the imposing Central Block and Eagle Block stood at the corner of South and West Main Streets. One of the first things passengers would see after arriving at the station were the stores and services in one central location. Groceries, furniture, watches, dry goods, and even banking were available. A year earlier, the Westborough Savings Bank opened its first office on the second floor.

The S.G. Henry and Company, an apothecary store that sold drugs and medicine, was also located in this block of stores. Dr. Henry not only ran the apothecary but was also the first practicing dentist in town. Just to the left of Dr. Henry's store was the Protection Union Store. All of these buildings were destroyed by fire on June 17, 1873.

In 1836, the Cobb Block, which was originally built as a shoe factory and later converted to house retail businesses, was constructed at West Main and Milk Streets. When this picture was taken in 1871, the town's newspaper, the *Chronotype*, was located on the upper floor, with boardinghouse rooms on the middle floor and a furniture store at ground level. Many different businesses occupied this building until it was demolished in 1935. The Post Office Block, erected in 1869 and demolished in 2013, is to the left.

This view from 1873 shows the old Arcade Building located on West Main Street between Milk and Summer Streets. Originally built as the Second Meeting House in 1748, it was sold in 1837 due to the noise of the railroad seriously interfering with the building's intended use. Luther Chamberlain purchased the building, removed the steeple, and raised the structure to add a new lower level. The building was demolished in 1890 and replaced with the current Arcade Building.

This photograph of West Main Street is from the 1870s, when wooden sidewalks and wide dirt streets were common in all small towns. All of the buildings on the left—from the center of town to the former Baptist church, including the town hall—have been demolished and replaced.

This West Main Street view is from the front of the old Arcade Building. The tree in front of the building was a popular gathering place, and the park benches provided a place for folks to rest and chat. Broadsides advertising shows at Chauncy Lake were posted on the screens. A wooden fountain provided water for the horses.

This 1870 picture was taken from the front of the town hall and looks toward the center of town. One of the old schoolhouses on the left was converted into a grocery store and butcher shop. The tower of the National Straw Works building on East Main Street is visible in the distance.

National Straw Works was incorporated in 1869. When this photograph was taken on March 20, 1878, there were about 2,000 workers employed on the company's assembly lines producing straw hats. Nineteen additional structures—for production, warehousing, and a rooming house—were constructed on the site at 9 East Main Street. In 1880, this was the largest straw-hat factory in the country. Sadly, the company came to a sudden end when it could not meet the demand for new styles and more fashionable hats. By 1899, National Straw Works was closed.

Westborough was known for three main industries: straw hats, sleigh building, and the manufacturing of shoes and boots. These were the leading manufacturers in town around the time of the late 19th century. Multiple companies produced these products and forever changed the character of the town. The Forbes Sleigh Factory, which was located on Summer Street, was among around 10 companies that built more than 4,500 sleighs in 1874.

The Gould and Walker Shoe Factory was located on the corner of Phillips and Milk Streets. In 1886, William R. Gould started construction—he soon employed more than 300 workers to produce more than 700 cases of shoes per week. Over a dozen other shoe manufacturers produced hundreds of thousands of shoes here until there was a disastrous fire in 1947; this factory and more than 20 other buildings and homes were damaged or destroyed.

The Rassmussen Shoe Company was still producing shoes until the 1947 fire. During World War II, Rasmussen was the primary contractor for the US Army in the production of mukluks—canvas and leather boots with heavy felt inserts that were about 18 inches tall. These were the preferred boot worn by US paratroopers and mountain troops during the war.

Westboro Trunk and Bag opened in 1899 and was located in the middle of the Staples Block on East Main Street. Suitcases and trunks became a necessity with the arrival of train travel that could transport a person anywhere in the country. For almost 20 years, more than 100 workers produced bags and trunks until the building was destroyed by fire in 1917.

The arrival of the Boston & Worcester Railroad brought many benefits to the town, but along with the good came the bad. Residents and merchants started to complain about the noise and frequency of trains traveling through the center of town. It was disrupting local church services, blocking local merchants from delivering their goods, and creating a hazard for pedestrians. The town and railroad agreed it would be best to relocate the tracks away from the center of town; therefore, in 1899, the tracks were moved to their current location.

The new train depot opened in 1899 and was an instant success. Passenger service direct to New York and Boston operated until it was discontinued in 1960. Freight trains continued to use the original railroad yards off Brigham Street. Six sidings with multiple freight houses were available to serve Westborough businesses with raw materials being shipped in and finished goods being shipped out.

The Adams Express Company was located on East Main Street near National Straw Works. In 1837, the company was started for the delivery of parcels between Worcester and Boston. It shipped most items by stagecoach until the railroad arrived. It also had carriers on bicycles who delivered messages and letters. By the 1920s, Adams Express had merged with another company and become the Railway Express Agency. Note the Humber Cycles sign on the side of the building.

In 1889, Frederick White opened the White Cycle Company in a newly constructed building at 12 Beach Street. In 1895, foreign interests in the booming US bicycle business purchased the building and began manufacturing Humber Bicycles. In the Westborough plant, Humber and Company started producing quality European bicycles that could be purchased for $125. The company closed in 1899, and the plant was converted to manufacture Locomobiles. That plant closed in 1902 and was converted to house the Westboro Tannery, which closed in 1969. The building was burned down in 1971 due to the possibility of anthrax spores.

The Post Office Block at 25 West Main Street was constructed in 1869 and demolished in 2014. Rooms for rent on the upper floors provided temporary housing for traveling salesmen visiting Westborough and surrounding towns. Various town organizations, including the Westborough Historical Society, had meeting rooms on the upper floors. The Westborough Post Office remained in this building until it relocated to a new facility on East Main Street in 1915.

The Whitney House was located at 45 West Main Street adjacent to Memorial Cemetery. Built in 1881 by Christopher Whitney, the hotel offered high-class accommodations and provided running hot and cold water, electric lights, and free transportation to the train station. Whitney also owned the local box factory and an impressive home on West Main Street.

In contrast to the Whitney House, the National House, located on East Main Street, catered to local factory workers. Eighteen inexpensive rooms with basic necessities were available to rent by the day or week. In later years, it became the Westborough Inn; it was destroyed by fire in 1917.

Westborough welcomed a new four-story brick building at 26 West Main Street in 1886. The Park Block became the new home of Frost Hardware Company. The signs above the doors indicated that a vast selection of china and glassware on display in the windows was available for purchase, as well as baby carriages, ice chests, lamps, and lanterns. The building is still standing today and is located to the left of the town hall on West Main Street.

The center of Westborough was the hub and connecting point for local trolley companies. This c. 1900 picture shows some of the different trolley lines converging in the center. Passengers could explore the J.S. Gates Store in the light-colored building or visit the C.S. Henry Drug Store in the brick building to the left. Tickets for various destinations could be purchased on the trolley or at the trolley waiting room in the Cobb Block at Milk and West Main Streets. By 1910, trolley cars

were available to take passengers directly to Boston from the Milk Street station near Turnpike Road. Changes were coming to Westborough when the Carlstrom Bus line started replacing the trolleys in 1921. Ten years later, buses were running on all the former trolley routes. A three-bay brick bus garage still exists today at 32 East Main Street.

On West Main Street, located to the right of the Post Office Block, sat another drugstore, the Buxton Rexall Store. The clerks were often referred to as the "Buxton Boys" and were known for their bright white attire. As this 1901 photograph shows, their white jackets were almost blinding. At the time this photograph was taken, there were three other drug or apothecary stores downtown.

The c. 1901 interior view of this drugstore shows typical items being sold in drugstores. On the left are a gumball dispenser and a large cigar display, along with the cash register and wrapping area. Along the back wall are bottles of medications; on the counter, a large display of postcards; and to the right is a small ice cream and soda fountain. On the near right, there are displays of personal products on the walls and counters.

Between the Post Office Block and the Cobb Block on West Main Street was Woodman's Hardware Store, which opened in 1887. The store sold stoves, hardware, farming tools, and assorted housewares. As at other Westborough stores, delivery was included with a purchase. The delivery wagon and a well-dressed driver in hat and tie are pictured in front of the store.

Most families did not have a wagon, so local grocery and dry goods stores, such as the F.C. Lamb Company located on South Street, delivered groceries to customers. Many families had only bicycles for transportation, but riding a bike was not feasible in the winter. It was more important to have a sleigh than a wagon to transport goods, as many items were sold in bulk in large wood barrels or tin boxes.

Located on the corner of Phillips and Milk Streets, the Hunt Company produced bicycle seats at this location prior to the building being purchased by the Westboro Hat Company in 1904. By the early 1900s, Westboro Hat Company was the primary manufacturer of straw hats in town. For almost 40 years, the company continued to produce various styles of hats, many of which were shipped as far away as the Midwest.

Near the Westboro Hat Company was the Westborough Weaving Company at 69 Milk Street. Built in 1902, the factory produced fabric and cloth tape that was used as the waistband on clothing. By 1930, the company had moved out of town, and the factory building was vacant until the 1940s, when a third floor was added. The building is still in use today and houses multiple independent businesses.

One of the many freight houses that stored goods to be shipped to and from Westborough was located off Brigham Street. Each day, up to four trains delivered freight cars here. A total of six railroad sidings could handle multiple cars being loaded and unloaded.

One of the issues facing manufacturers in Westborough was being able to ensure that their merchandise arrived intact. Items transported by rail needed to be securely boxed in order to prevent damage during shipping. In 1870, Christopher Whitney opened a lumber operation called the Bartlett Box Company on Union Street in the center of the freight yard. The company provided wooden crates used to ship all types and sizes of merchandise—from bicycles to sleighs. It was one of the most profitable businesses in town until it closed in the 1930s.

No one knew the impact the railroad would have on the little village of Westborough. The train brought manufacturing, hospitality, and retail and grocery stores to this former farming community. Residents could buy items they had to grow in the past and purchase clothes that were normally made at home. Life would improve greatly when electricity finally arrived.

When passengers arrived at the train station in the center of town, they saw a community leading the way into the future. The unemployed could find decent jobs and housing, and businessmen found a steady workforce and a community that welcomed them. In 1889, the Westboro Board of Trade summed it up best by stating, "To all who are looking for a location for a business, to all who desire a home in a pleasant town, to all who appreciate a healthful summer residence that they inspect for themselves the numerous advantages by the Town of Westborough."

Seven

Fires and Disasters

In 1888, the town voted to build an engine house; this photograph was taken after it was completed a year later. The *Chronotype* gave the following description of the new structure: "The building is of brick with granite trimmings. It is a handsome and imposing looking building on its exterior, and the interior is also handsome, roomy and convenient." This building served the town for more than 125 years before being replaced in 2014.

The new building was heated by a Spence hot water system with radiators on the upper floors, and the first floor was heated by pipes. Electric lights were installed throughout the entire station. The inside of the engine house had one large room on the ground floor that measured 45 by 50 feet. For the first time, all the independent companies—the Jackson Steamer Company, Rescue Hook and Ladder Company, William Curtis Hose Company, and Chauncy Hose Company—would be housed under one roof, with each company having its own meeting room upstairs. The exception was the Young American Bucket Company, which remained independent of the town. The company consisted of 20 members who had 24 water buckets and 50 feet of ladders. The Young American Bucket Company was always on alert and ready to render all the assistance they could provide.

In 1868, the town purchased a steamer from Hunneman and Company for the Jackson Steamer Company's 20 men. Once a notice about a fire was received, members of the company started a fire in the boiler, and the horses were brought from the stable and connected to the steamer. The horses made good time to the scene. There were 12 brick reservoirs in different parts of town with a capacity of 200 hogsheads each (a hogshead equals 79 gallons of water). Once the company members had arrived, the steamer would pump the water onto the fire.

On June 17, 1873, the center of Westborough was filled with smoke and flames as the Central Block, Eagle Block, and Protective Union Store were all destroyed by fire. A local blacksmith, Antonio Joan, was convicted of setting the fire and sentenced to life in prison. Fire companies from as far away as Worcester came to the town to assist in putting out the fire.

In 1879, the town purchased property from Frank Sandra for a reservoir. The purchase increased the efficiency of the fire department via the water provided by Sandra Pond and the installation of 79 hydrants throughout the town. In the background is the town poor farm, which assisted the town's indigent from 1881 to 1948, when it was sold.

In 1887, the town purchased a replacement ladder truck for $800. The Rescue Hook and Ladder Company's 17 men finally had a reliable truck equipped with ladders, pike poles, hooks, and axes. This was the most elite of the various fire companies in Westborough.

In 1881, Christopher Whitney built the Whitney House hotel. This upper-class hotel provided travelers and salesmen with big, bright rooms on the three upper floors. A grocery store, dry goods store, and drugstore were on the ground floor. A livery and stable with a blacksmith were located in the rear. At the time of its construction, this was the most impressive building in Westborough.

In 1907, the Whitney House building was destroyed by a fire that was initially reported to have been caused by a kerosene lantern exploding over a pool table on the upper floor. This is a little odd, as the building was equipped with electric lights that Christopher Whitney and Henry Taft were instrumental in bringing to Westborough. Firefighters were able to save the surrounding homes along with the livery and stable.

After the Whitney House fire, much debris littered the lot—to the dismay of many townspeople. Fannie Forbes thought the debris was unsightly and did not best represent the town. The hotel was never rebuilt, so the Forbes family purchased the property to build a new high school; in 1926, they donated it to the town.

Even with the new reservoir and hydrant system, firefighters still had water problems. In this 1897 photograph of a public demonstration, multiple fire streams are visible. The main issue was that the pipes coming from Sandra Pond to the downtown area were too small to deliver an adequate water supply in the event of a major fire. This issue remained until the great fire of 1947.

The Chauncy Hose Company was comprised of 15 men who came from all walks of life. The majority of them worked at Westboro Hat Company, while others were employed in one of the sleigh factories or boot shops. They were called to action by the blowing of the steam whistle at the National Straw Works and the ringing of the bells on the Baptist and Congregational churches. The company's equipment consisted of a hand-drawn hose cart and 500 feet of hose with two nozzles.

The 20 firefighters in the William Curtis Hose Company were a little older and more experienced. There was always competition regarding which the company could pull its hose cart toward the fire the fastest. More than once, a trolley car was commandeered to pull the hose cart and transport the firefighters toward the inferno.

On May 11, 1908, the downtown area was hit with another disastrous fire. A small fire broke out in the warehouse of the Foster-Richardson Bedstead Factory on Cottage Street. The fire started in the warehouse and soon destroyed more than 1,000 beds that had been prepared for shipment. The fire spread beyond the warehouse and destroyed two rooming houses and the Armour Beef warehouse.

The fire department quickly arrived at the scene of the 1908 fire. On the upper floors of the warehouse, beds were packed tightly with flammable excelsior in preparation for shipping. Again, the town discovered that there was not enough water to supply more than four hose lines at any one time. Business owners were becoming angry at the lack of a proper water supply.

The 1908 fire also spread to several small warehouses that contained plumbing supplies and merchandise waiting to be shipped by railroad car. Two firefighters were thrown to the ground when their wooden ladder broke, but according to the local paper, they were not seriously injured, as they landed in a pile of ashes.

Many buildings were destroyed by fire in the late 19th century. In Westborough, one of the causes was determined to be a local arsonist who was never caught. Most buildings were heated by wood or coal, so chimney fires were common. Not every building had electric lights, so kerosene lanterns and candles were still being used. Even the new electric lights sometimes short-circuited and caused fires. Fire prevention was not something that most factory owners practiced.

In 1910, the Jackson Steamer Company was called to a large fire in the adjacent town of Woodville. The steamer raced to the scene and arrived in 11 minutes to find the offices and showroom of the L.E. Coolidge Company fully ablaze. The steamer was of little use, as there was no water nearby. The building was a total loss, but the firefighters were able to save the barn and stable.

After a fire, there was quite a lot of cleaning up to be done. There was always a group of young boys who were ready to pitch in and help out the firefighters. In this view, there is not much left of the building, and the fire hose has been damaged and burnt. The boys may have been hoping that one day, they could become members of the fire department and actually fight fires.

At approximately 10:00 a.m. on June 21, 1907, came a thundering crash. It was so loud that the *Westborough Chronotype* described it as "the roar of a cannon." Smoke and steam could be seen in the distance east of the new passenger train station. As residents flocked to the scene, they encountered a horrific train wreck.

The *New York Express* passenger train collided with a freight train roughly 300 feet east of the new passenger station on June 21, 1907. The express train's engineer saw the freight train and applied the brakes, but it was too late. The railroad had failed to send out a flagman to warn approaching trains that the track was occupied.

At the scene of the train collision on June 21, 1907, the engineer and fireman remained with the engine as it overturned but were able to crawl out and sustained only minor injuries. The passengers were somewhat shaken, and some of the female passengers were greatly overwhelmed with fright, according to local accounts. Dr. Clark and Dr. Ayer responded with their medical bags but were not needed, as there were no deaths and only a few minor injuries. The track was littered with remains of the destroyed boxcars, and the rails were torn from the railroad ties. The new steam engine (which was only on its second trip) and tender were destroyed. It took the railroad several days to dismantle and remove the twisted metal, which provided an interesting distraction for those viewing the wreckage.

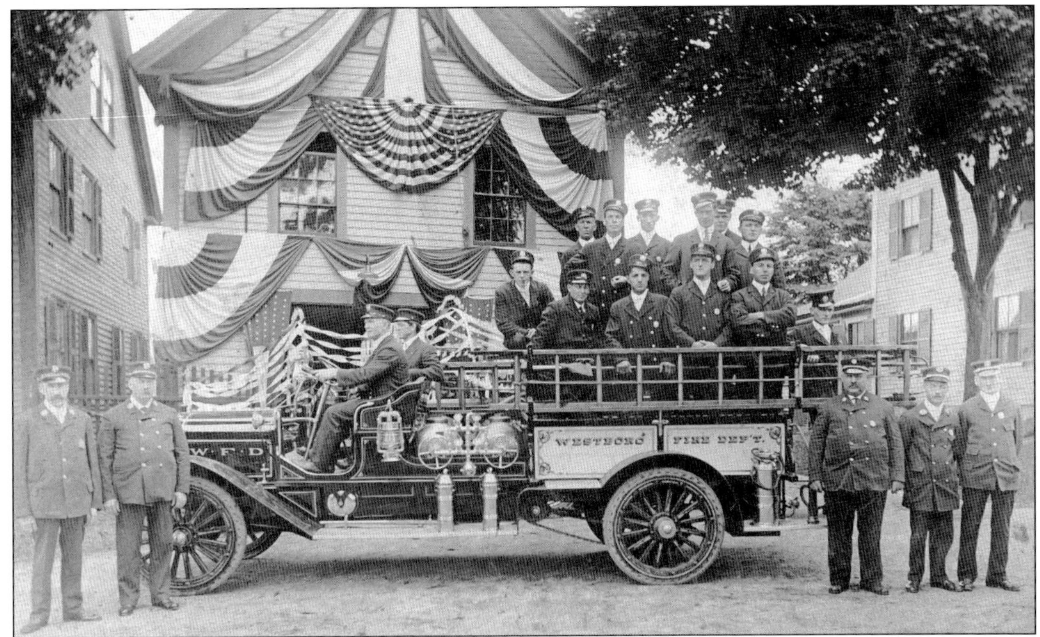

By 1912, travel by horse was being replaced as gasoline engines in automobiles and trucks became the norm. The Westborough Fire Department modernized its fleet by purchasing its first motor-driven fire apparatus in 1914. The fire truck was a Brockway chemical truck, and it was a chain drive. It carried 200 gallons of water in two pressurized tanks, which made it perfect for small fires.

The new fire engine was of little use on October 12, 1917. Due to high winds that day, a fire started to spread quickly in the Westborough Trunk and Bag Company, which was located in this building that once housed the National Straw Works. It would take nearly a week for the smoke and flames to finally die out and clear.

The morning after the October 1917 fire went out, the residents could view the devastation left by the conflagration. Hundreds of jobs were lost, and 11 buildings were destroyed or damaged. Westborough had seen many fires, but no one was prepared for this. Assistance arrived from as far away as Worcester, which sent fire trucks on rail cars to the train station.

All that remained after the October 1917 fire were the smokestacks; nothing was able to be salvaged from the debris. The tremendous heat damaged the electric lines on East Main Street, and after several days, power was restored to parts of the center of town. The town's water supply was depleted; consequently, it took several days before water again ran from the taps.

The October 1917 fire was allowed to burn itself out; any remaining water needed to be saved for another potential fire. Fortunately for the town, the direction of the wind had changed, and the fire was blown directly onto the new Keating Block, which was considered fireproof due to its brick facade. The entire center of Westborough could have been destroyed.

The buildings that were destroyed in the October 1917 fire included the Staples Block, which was home to several small businesses: the Westborough Inn, formally the National House; the Hassell Lace Curtain Factory; and Westborough Trunk and Bag Company. Two warehouses and a small blacksmith shop were also destroyed.

The Keating Block, also known as the Oddfellows Building, was credited with stopping the great Westborough fire in October 1917. The fire stopped here because the block was built from brick. Although the building did catch fire, firefighters working inside were able to put out the flames as the windows exploded. The building also housed the town's post office, and no mail was damaged.

The devastation caused by the October 1917 fire is visible in this image. The broken and missing windows in the Keating Building were caused by the intense flames. This fire led the town to give some consideration to better fire protection for its citizens and businesses. The first step was to hire Westborough's first full-time paid firefighter. Edward Hogan was hired to work seven days a week and was allowed two days off each month.

The town also purchased two additional fire pumpers. In 1918, a Maxim pumper was acquired, followed by another Maxim pumper a few years later. Soon, the familiar blast of the steam whistles would be phased out and replaced by the loud blast of a pair of powerful air horns on top of the fire station. The sound could be heard from miles away.

Another fire engine added to the fleet was specifically to be used for forest fires. This engine was equipped with a pump that could be removed and set up in a pond or stream and a small-diameter hose designed for brush fires. The fire equipment was improving and keeping up with the needs of a growing town.

The town still refused to upgrade the water system after the October 1917 fire. Downtown hydrants were few and provided little water. In 1947, as the former Westboro Hat Company and Gould and Walker (a.k.a. the Hat Shop and the Boot Shop) burned, firefighters could do little except watch. More than 20 buildings were either destroyed or damaged by this fire, including the fire station.

By the time of the 1947 fire, the town had a new fire station, modern equipment, and a full-time firefighter. The most important issue that needed to be rectified was the lack of an adequate water supply. It took the devastating 1947 blaze for the town to react and build a network of high-pressure water lines, new hydrants, and a storage tank. This system is still in place today.

Eight

Townsfolk

Photographers will admit that pictures of people are much more interesting than those of buildings. They provide a snapshot of time and can transport us back to the exact instant the photograph was taken. The photographer conveys a story through an image. Westborough was unusual, as there were more than 15 commercial photographers in the center of town during the 1890s. This image shows Abigale Crowe playing piano at a home located at 95 East Main Street that was demolished in the 1970s.

Everyday life was recorded for future generations by local photographers. Little did they know that the images they captured would be so important a century later. Historians and scholars can examine the most minute detail for any important historical significance. From the signs on the buildings to the bystanders on the street, every picture has a story to tell. This picture taken by F.E. North captures Ebeneza Lincoln returning home to Grafton after visiting Westborough.

On a nice summer day in 1895, the Westborough Historical Society traveled to Shrewsbury in a caravan of wagons and horses to visit the historic Artemas Ward House. Incorporated on February 28, 1889, with 23 charter members, the society was founded to investigate matters of local history, collect objects of historical and scientific interest, and maintain a library. The society is now located in the William Sibley House at 13 Parkman Street.

Some of the rarest photographs are of people performing their daily routines. Outside the controlled light of a photography studio, photographers faced the challenges of varied weather and environments. Pictured here is a local resident with his small collection of pigs and chickens; this was typical for many families in Westborough at the time.

Another resident is shown bringing eggs into his farmhouse. The collection of empty milk cans drying outside was a common sight for those who had the luxury of owning their own cow. Many residents did not have the time to farm as they worked in the factories, so they relied on the local dry goods and grocery stores for their food. On occasion, a farmer would trade milk and eggs with a neighbor for goods or services.

In 1881, the Grand Army of the Republic Post No. 80 was formed with 51 charter members. Six years later, in 1887, the Frank L. Stone Encampment, also known as the Sons of the Civil War Veterans, was organized with 36 members. Both of these philanthropic organizations were well known for tending to elderly and injured veterans in town. These fiercely proud groups were always at the front of parades and civic functions.

In the late 1890s, another interesting group was the Westborough Clam Club, not to be confused with the Westborough Ketch-um and Fry-um Fish Club. As the name suggests, the group traveled to Cape Cod and the South Shore to dig for clams. It was an all-day affair to travel by horse and wagon to their destinations. On occasion, they would travel by train to Boston and then by trolley to their favorite clamming locations.

Not everyone enjoyed the outdoors, especially in the winter months. Some staff at the Lyman School are shown in this candid photograph relaxing with a game of cards. Board and card games were the primary types of indoor recreation in the 1890s. It would take another generation before radio stations would arrive.

In the 1890s, it was not yet socially acceptable for women to play cards, except with their husbands. These card-playing women were on an outside porch on Church Street when this photograph was taken. Even though playing cards had been around for more than 400 years at this point, they still were not acceptable entertainment for respectable women of the day.

Here is a more acceptable—for the time—image of the Victorian women shown in the previous photograph. They are impeccably dressed in ornate dresses, gloves, and wonderful hats. The table is adorned with a tablecloth, teapot, sugar, and creamer as these ladies enjoy their tea time. Many women worked as hard as their husbands on the farms, and many worked in the factories as well.

Baseball was a popular pastime in town. Many of the factories had teams that would compete against each other on a regular basis. The team shown here included workers from the Fraser Machine Shop; some of the members are wearing Westborough High School jerseys. The manager, Bill Ford, is on the far right on the second row (with the straw hat), and the young boy sitting in front is Leo Cassinari, who was the team mascot.

Westborough High School had only ten graduates in 1895—two men and eight women. All graduates from the class of 1895 went on to college. Most young men left school early to help out on the farm or to go to work in one of the factories. These two images were found in an old scrapbook with the caption, "A survival of the fittest." The first Westborough High School opened on Science Hill in 1854 after the land was donated by local resident Draper Ruggles. Classes included grammar, geography, bookkeeping, mental philosophy, natural philosophy, chemistry, physiology, improvement of the mind, rhetoric, astronomy, arithmetic, algebra, geometry, trigonometry, surveying, history, Latin, Greek, composition, and declaration.

Sometimes an image tells more than a description. This picture of the Lyman School Band was taken in 1887. The young faces are devoid of smiles. Many of the boys sent here were from broken homes or were discarded and left on city streets to survive. Some found their way to the Lyman School, which proved to be a difficult place to endure. However, the boys would receive a warm

meal, some education, and learn the meaning of discipline, hard work, and perhaps a trade. For many of the boys, this system worked. The major problems stemmed from boys ranging in age from 9 to 18 being housed together, but an attempt was made to keep the younger boys separate from the older boys, with some success.

The Supreme Council of the Royal Arcanum was another fraternal society in Westborough. Headquartered in Boston, the organization had more than 200,000 members by 1896. This outing was held at Chauncy Park around 1890. The Supreme Council of the Royal Arcanum, commonly referred to as the Royal Arcanum, is still active today as a fraternal benefit society. The streetcar operator on the left looks quite impressive dressed in his full uniform.

This undated photograph was taken on Memorial Day in front of the old town hall on West Main Street. The Grand Army of the Republic men and the Relief Corps ladies gathered for this image. One of the identified individuals is Noah Trank, who is third from the left in the second row. Trank operated a local shoe store on South Street for many years before retiring.

Pine Grove Cemetery, located on South Street, opened in 1844 and still is in use today. In this 1890 image, several children are at the entrance; two of the boys appear to be playing a game of marbles. All of the patients who passed away at Westborough State Hospital whose remains were not claimed are buried in the babies' and paupers' section of this cemetery.

In this undated photograph, it is known that the subjects are teachers thanks to a note on the negative. The woman second from right in the first row, with her eyes closed, is wearing a Westboro Band hat; perhaps she was the town's music teacher.

The two little boys standing under the gate of the grand entrance leading to the Whitney Estate are the Whitney brothers. Located at 90 West Main Street, this was the largest and most elaborate estate in town. The original estate ran the entire length of West Main Street from Charles Street and behind the houses on West Main to Chestnut Street. O'Neil Drive was originally referred to as Whitney Hill.

This 1880s photograph shows a Westborough family who could afford a photographer to take portraits at their home. The bright outside lighting permitted the photographer to set his camera on a faster shutter speed; this allowed people to pose for a shorter time, which made it less likely that they would move and blur the photograph. The subjects are all serious, as was typical at the time, because it was easier for a person to hold a serious face than a smiling face.

Before Frank and Fannie Forbes purchased the property and built Kirkside at 8 Church Street, there were magnificent gardens and a summer house on the site. The Trowbridge family had a large home and extensive gardens with small ponds and walkways. More than 1,000 different species were said to be growing on the site, and during the summer, a strong smell of lavender filled the Church Street neighborhood. The gardens remained until 1917, when the Forbeses constructed Kirkside, a magnificent home designed for the elderly who had little or no income, and all expenses were paid by the Forbes family. Kirkside was closed and sold to the Congregational Church in 1950. In 2013, the church sold the property to Right at Home, a company that provides senior care and elder assistance.

Most small towns had a gathering place, and Westborough was no different. The large beech tree in front of the old Arcade Building was a local hangout. Advertising broadsides were posted on the fence, and the benches provided a comfortable place where people could exchange pleasantries and gossip. Formal attire was optional for the mosquito fleet seated here.

The property at 89 West Main Street, across from Westborough High School, is the backdrop of this charming photograph of a little boy pulling a wagon in which a young girl is sitting. Another little girl is at the front door to the house with her carriage. The image may have been commissioned by the children's parents.

It was a good day for hunting for this local resident—accompanied by his faithful dog—with a shotgun in one hand and a pheasant in the other. Hunting deer, duck, and even rabbit was necessary for many of the townspeople to provide food for their families.

For more than 125 years, children have congregated at the Soldier's Monument and fountain at Memorial Cemetery across from the town hall. The monument was erected in 1868 as a memorial recognizing the sacrifice of local residents. The fountain has been restored, and in the summer, water still flows from it every day.

The Grand Army of the Republic block, which housed several small merchants on the ground level, was located on South Street. On the right was a store for gentlemen. Shirts and bowler hats are on display in the window. There were many similar small shops in the center of town.

This photograph was taken on the grounds of the Whitney Estate on West Main Street. The property was gigantic and contained more than 100 acres. These two individuals appear to be relaxing outside one of the numerous buildings on the property. The young boy may be one of the Whitney boys.

Nine

Historic Homes

At the corner of High and East Main Streets sits a classic Greek Revival–style house. According to town records, this home at 30 East Main Street was built around 1800. Closer to the railroad tracks in this 1900 photograph are two additional homes that are no longer standing.

Eli Whitney's birthplace was located at 36 Eli Whitney Street. The original house was built in the early 1720s and torn down in 1853. The land was sold by Eli Whitney's nephew to Marcus Grout, who erected the home currently on the site (pictured) in 1850. The only item remaining from the original house is the granite doorstep that is now displayed in the front yard with a bronze plaque.

There are only seven homes on Lincoln Street, and this was the first—1 Lincoln Street, built around 1870. To this day, the house appears remarkably unchanged except for the large wraparound porch that was added later. The large barn in the rear was removed at some unknown point.

The property at 13 High Street is one of the more beautiful and colorful houses on the street. The house remains true to its original design and elaborate paint scheme. This early 1890s photograph was taken from State Street and shows a new home with no trees or gardens. A street sign partially visible on the far left side of the image warns that this private way is dangerous.

West Main Street has more early historic homes still remaining than any other street in town. The house at 69 West Main Street was built around 1795—minus the front porch entryway—and is a survivor. Many of the town's older homes were either destroyed by fire or neglected and fell into disrepair. The three women on West Street seem to be interested in the photographer's activities.

This house at 72 South Street, pictured here in the 1890s, has an interesting history and, according to town records, was first occupied in 1777. Once owned by the family of Rev. Ebenezer Parkman, the structure was known as the Breck Parkman Shop. Originally located downtown near the old Post Office Block, the building housed a small store and the residence of the Parkman family. It was moved to the corner of Summer and East Main Streets about 1855. Eight years later, it was loaded onto a set of wheels and moved to Milk Street near Phillips Street. Before it could be unloaded, it was purchased by Patrick Cronican in 1865 and moved to 72 South Street. In 1940, the house was replaced with a new structure similar in style to the original. The family and house are referenced in *The Parkman Diaries*, published by the Westborough Historical Society in 1899.

The house on the left is 3 Fay Street, built around 1800; this single-family house has been converted to a three-family apartment building. Many of the large homes in downtown Westborough have been converted to multifamily apartments or condominiums. The home at right is at 76 Milk Street; built around 1890, it has also been converted to a multifamily dwelling. Both houses still retain unique features from their original construction.

Two other historic homes are located at 54 and 56 West Main Street. The light-colored Colonial was built around 1815 and is now a multifamily building with 17 rooms. The darker Victorian was built in 1884 and remains a single-family residence. Both homes have had some renovations over the years.

The Haskell House is one of the oldest homes in town. Timothy Warren sold land located at the corner of East Main and Haskell Streets to Thomas Chase in 1756. Chase constructed a house and a blacksmith shop, and in 1764, he sold the property to Phineas Haskell, who was a farmer and a blacksmith. Haskell did not care to get involved with the business of the town and kept to himself. He labored to improve his property with fruit trees and berries, and it is recorded that the neighborhood children enjoyed the results of his labor. The property consisted of many acres, and in 1842, a plot containing approximately 40 acres was sold to Nathan Fisher. Although the house had been in the possession of the Haskell family for almost 140 years, it was sold in 1901, because no family members were interested in occupying the house. As with many old homes, children were born and family members passed on here; the inhabitants of the Haskell House welcomed 20 births and mourned 13 deaths.

Across from Westborough High School on West Main Street stands a large Colonial home. Before this home was built in 1835, the property was owned by Deacon Joseph Newton, who was one of the most influential and important characters in the early days of Westborough. Deacon Newton wore many hats in his lifetime—he was the deacon of the Congregational church for almost 20 years, and he found time to be the town clerk, town selectman, and meeting moderator. A Newton family member also figured prominently in King Philip's War after being injured by Native Americans. In 1715, Deacon Newton purchased 32 acres of land from Thomas Rice, which led to the original Newton farm extending from Church Street to the current site of the Westborough Country Club on West Main Street. The property changed hands several more times and was eventually sold by the Blake family; Josiah Blake divided the land into house lots and laid out the street that became known as Blake Street.

At the corner of Central and West Main Streets stands another Westborough landmark. Constructed prior to 1900, this building has housed guests for over 100 years. Known as the "Merrie M" to residents since at least the 1940s, it has provided rooms and refreshments for weary travelers. It was also well known for its tea room that provided afternoon tea and homemade refreshments.

At 52 West Main Street, next door to the "Merrie M," is another grand residence similar to the other early homes in Westborough. This was originally built as a single-family home around 1830, and very little has changed on the structure; even the small attached shed in the rear remains.

The house at 114 East Main Street was built around 1730 and demolished in 2011 due to the declining condition of the structure. It was the home of Tom Cook, the Westborough Robin Hood and a local patriot instrumental in preparing Westborough for the Revolutionary War. Dr. James Hawes, the original owner, delivered a document to Boston in 1773 stating the rights of the colonists. Dr. Hawes was authorized to transport this document after a meeting of Westborough residents. In addition, he was appointed to a committee in 1774 to purchase the following: a field piece (cannon), a four-pounder (artillery gun), and 400 weight of ball (lead balls) with 10 half-barrels of powder, 500 weight of lead (for bullets), and flints. Dr. Hawes continued to serve the town as town officer from 1775 to 1786, town moderator in 1782, town clerk in 1776, town treasurer from 1797 to 1798, and state representative from 1778 to 1780.

East Main Street has been the site of the razing of quite a few historic homes over the years. Around 1890, this home was built at 24 East Main Street; it was replaced by a Mobil service station in 1962. The author was witness to the demolition of this home and sat on the granite curb on High Street while the house was dismantled and removed.

School Street looks out on an impressive row of Colonial homes on West Main Street. All of the homes in this 1880s photograph still have families residing in them. The white Colonial home on the far right still has the white picket fence around the house. All of these homes were built sometime between 1770 and 1830.

The house in this photograph was built by S. Deane Fisher, one of the original founders of the Westborough Agricultural Society. In 1856, he sold the house and 74 acres of land on Milk Street to James Robinson, who named the homestead "Robinsonia." The land was developed into apple orchards after Robinson purchased it.

These two homes stood at the intersection of Milk and Fisher Streets. The one on the left is at 85 Milk Street, and the other is at 83 Milk Street; both were built before 1900. They still retain their New England charm in spite of a few changes to 85 Milk Street, including the removal of the large glass sunroom and the addition of a porch.

This Colonial at 64 Warren Street will be 300 years old in 2020. Built in 1720, the historic home looks a little worse for wear in this c. 1889 image. Most of the whitewash has faded off the house, and the bare wood is exposed. Today, the house is stunning, with a restoration that maintained the unique exterior features of the home.

Church Street is home to some of the most beautifully restored homes in town. One fine example is the home at 45 Church Street (on the left), which was built around 1890. The house at right, located at 43 Church Street, was completely restored in the 2010s and was recently on the market for $1.75 million. Built in 1855, the 43 Church Street house is impressive inside and out.

This picture of 87 West Main Street was taken from across the street at the entrance to the Whitney Estate around the time it was built in 1893. This house recently sold and has returned to being a private home after serving as a bed and breakfast. Most features of this building remain intact, including the wonderful eyebrow windows on the roof.

The Parkman's Farmers' House was built prior to 1782 and located on the farm of Rev. Ebenezer Parkman at High and East Main Streets. It is documented that local farmers Parkman had hired to work the farm lived in this house. It was eventually acquired by the Boston & Albany Railroad and torn down in 1907.

Church Street is lined with historic homes, including this house at 37 Church Street. Built as a single-family home in 1896, it has been converted to four apartments. It still retains some of its original features, including the front porch and the unique windows on the third floor.

The structure at 172 West Main Street is an antique farmhouse. Built in 1730, the home is set back from the street and continues to serve its original purpose. Built as a single-family home, it has been converted to a two-family residence and is currently on the property of the Wilkinson Hi-Hill Farm.

This old workshop was located behind 40 South Street. The house in front was newer—built about 1870. The workshop is historic—not because of the building, but because of what occurred inside it. According to local newspaper reports, on June 11, 1919, this peaceful neighborhood in Westborough was suddenly home to a flurry of commotion when news spread about a murder. An eccentric old recluse had been murdered, and the chief suspects were a woman known as "Baby Doll" (Eleanor Baker) and her husband, Harry Baker. They quickly vanished after the body of Dwight Chapman was found with his head beaten with a hammer. It was determined that robbery was the motive. The police quickly gathered leads and trailed the suspects as far north as Portland, Maine. When they were finally cornered in Bangor, Baby Doll pulled a gun, but the police prevailed. This picture is from a collection of the original crime scene photographs taken by the police. The story was so sensational that it was written up in several crime magazines over the next 10 years and remains a topic of interest today.

This historic home is located at 88 West Main Street. Christopher Whitney purchased the land and the existing home on the site in 1851 and transformed it into a 15-room grand mansion. Situated on a large plot of land, the property was filled with manicured lawns and gardens. The estate ran the entire length of West Main Street (behind existing homes) from Charles Street to Chestnut Street. The gardens and grounds extended as far back as Ruggles Street, and the property contained an impressive barn, numerous outbuildings, and a springhouse. The Whitney family enjoyed the home for many years, and it remained a showplace, with its lavish steel and wooden arch over the main entrance. The home stayed in the family; in 1889, it was passed on to Christopher Whitney's daughter and her husband, Frank Bartlett, and they sold it to the Aronson family. On June 9, 1953, the home was destroyed by an F4 tornado, and three people died at the scene. The home was never rebuilt and is now the site of Westborough High School.

Ten

Odds and Ends

This photograph of a window full of ribbon candy at Wichenbach's Store in the Cobb Block at West Main and Milk Streets is from January 1910. On this real-photo postcard, the owner commented, "We made 8,000 pounds of Xmas candy and kept up on the other kinds made. Made a barrel of kisses for a man for him to take on the trolley."

The new Westborough Public Library opened in June 1908. In this image, the building is still in the construction phase, with piles of loam on the front lawn. The library was the pride of the village when it was finished, and it housed almost 1,300 books. One of the library's unique features was a frosted-glass floor supported by a steel frame in the book stacks.

The Forbes and Curtis Grammar Schools on Grove Street were demolished in 1905. The following year, they were replaced with the Eli Whitney School, which housed grades three through six. This view shows the Eli Whitney School building under construction. In January 2000, the building was considered surplus and sold to the YMCA of Central Massachusetts.

The town hall was constructed in 1839, after the meetinghouse was sold, and held the town offices, library, and police department. This photograph of the old town hall was taken in 1885 from the end of Underwood Court. Starting in the 1870s, the First District Court held sessions here three days a week. The local fire department housed the rescue hook and ladder truck in the basement, and the original fire barn that housed steamer No. 2 is visible to the left of the building. The upstairs auditorium was in constant use for town meetings, movies, plays, and dances. The building was remodeled several times but could not meet the needs of a growing town. Ninety years after the town hall shown here was built, the Forbes family contributed the majority of funds to construct the current town hall, which was dedicated in 1929.

Everyone loves a parade, and Westborough was no different, as shown in this 1911 picture. Field Days always started with a parade featuring numerous floats and marching bands. Multiple parades were held in town every year, and the grandest was usually the Westborough Board of Trade Parade and Field Day. Road races were held, with the fastest runner winning an impressive trophy. There were numerous events at Chauncy Park, frequently followed by a large family picnic.

The members of this band preferred to stay anonymous behind their outlandish masks and long work coats. Pictured in front of the old town hall in 1911, this was one of the bands that performed in the Westborough Board of Trade Parade. To the left of the town hall was the bandstand, where residents would gather on Saturday nights to watch numerous local bands perform.

Automobiles were starting to replace the horse around the time this picture was taken at the 1912 Westborough Board of Trade Parade. At the time, it was uncommon to see automobiles in Westborough, so residents who could afford motorized vehicles showed them off in the parade. This photograph was taken in the center of town, with the Arcade Building in the background.

This young man is standing at the corner of Summer and East Main Streets. Behind him is the sign of a local blacksmith: "Eli Gaucher—Horseshoeing." Many farmers had summer and winter shoes for their horses. Horses could slip and fall on the ice on the ponds, so they had to wear horseshoes with spikes.

This 1886 image provides quite an expansive view of the downtown area. The Spurr House, located at 7 Parkman Street, is visible to the left of the large white rooming house. The First Methodist Church's steeple is visible on Milk Street; the church was built in 1864, and in 1897, it was sold to the grange. The smoke in the middle of the image is from one of the many steam engines that ran on the railroad track parallel to Milk Street until the track was relocated in 1899. The noise and smoke were contributing factors that led to the decision to sell the church. The Gould and Walker Shoe Factory, located at the corner of Milk and Phillips Streets, is the large five-story building at far left. In 1890, approximately 300 people were employed at this factory. A new fire station was built at the corner of Milk and Grove Streets two years after this photograph was taken.

This home at 121 West Main Street was built in the late 1890s. In this 1920s picture, "Westboro Country Club" is visible on the sign that is adorned with a large turkey on the top—an acknowledgment of the creatures that roamed the area. This property was known as Fox and Turkey Hills for the wild turkeys that made these hills and fields their home. On Memorial Day in 1921, the club formally opened with great fanfare and a clambake featuring clams and bluefish for members and their guests. At the time it opened, the club featured a nine-hole golf course and also provided residents with clay tennis courts and an area for lawn games. The 109-acre country club was sold to Bay State Abrasives in 1945, and in 1974, it was purchased by the town. It remains a popular spot for winter sports and has a highly rated nine-hole golf course.